Sing with Joy

compiled by
Paul Herrington, Roger Mayor
and David Peacock

Marshall Pickering

Music in Worship Trust

Preface

'Sing with Joy' is an exciting publication, the first to be produced by Music in Worship Trust. There are a considerable number of musicians nowadays involved with Christian worship who are looking for material which reflects the beauty and breadth of the character of God; but they wish to express their adoration and praise in many different ways.

So here is a book which offers scope for enterprising choirs e.g. *Psalm of Faith*; and it offers items for choirs and music groups who wish to accompany some of the many fine modern worship songs with contemporary vocal arrangements e.g. *All heaven declares, Shine Jesus Shine, Glory*. There are a few entirely new pieces written especially for this book such as *Come, light of the world* and *Unto him who is able*. There is some relatively simple music with which we can just enjoy ourselves in the Lord's presence; and there is material for the organist and choir who wish to offer a colourful ending to a hymn such as *Guide me, O my great Redeemer*.

This collection is a joint production between Music in Worship Trust and Marshall Pickering and published with support from the Pratt Green Trust.

We hope the book will give great pleasure to those who are looking for variety and a means through which they can lead their fellowships and congregations into the 'singing and making melody in our hearts to the Lord.'

Robin Sheldon
Director
Music in Worship Trust

Contents

All heaven declares	2
Away in a manger	10
Benediction	57
Come among us, Lord	7
Come, light of the world	14
Glory	29
Guide me, O my great Redeemer	18
He is not dead	20
I will sing of your love and justice	26
Invocations	14
Lord, you are the light of life	43
Lord, the light of your love	34
Psalm of Faith	46
Shine, Jesus, shine	34
There is a green hill	40
The Lord is my shepherd	46
Sing with joy	54
Unto him who is able	57

Orchestral/rhythm backing tracks on cassette are available for the following titles:

All heaven declares
Come among us, Lord
He is not dead
Lord, the light of your love (*Shine, Jesus, shine*)
There is a green hill
Unto him who is able (*Benediction*)

Side one of the cassette contains full settings of the items with singers accompanied by orchestra and band.

Instrumental parts are available as follows:

All heaven declares
   Violins I & II, violas, cellos, flute, B♭ trumpet, bass guitar

Come among us, Lord
   Violins I & II, violas, cellos, flute, clarinet, french horn

He is not dead
   Trumpets in B♭ I & II (or clarinets), alto saxophone, synthesiser, bass guitar

Lord, the light of your love (*Shine, Jesus, shine*)
   Violins I & II, violas, cellos, flute, B♭ clarinet, B♭ trumpets I & II, bass guitar, percussion (timpani, cymbal, bell-tree)

There is a green hill
   Violins I & II, violas, cellos, flute, bass guitar

Unto him who is able (*Benediction*)
   Violins I & II, violas, cellos, flute, clarinet, alto saxophone, bass guitar

Backing tracks and instrumental parts are available from:
Music in Worship Trust, 151 Bath Road, Hounslow, Middlesex TW3 3BU

All heaven declares

Festival arrangement for choir and congregation

Words and music: Noel and Tricia Richards
arranged Roger Mayor

Orchestral backing track (cassette) and instrumental parts available from Music in Worship Trust.

Copyright © 1987 Thankyou Music, PO Box 75, Eastbourne BN23 6NW, UK. Used by permission.

Come among us, Lord

Words: Gordon Brattle
Music: Robin Sheldon

Suggested options a. sing through as written
b. sing from letter B unaccompanied 1st time
c. sing from letter B in unison 1st or 2nd time
d. play piano as for vocal part from B

Music: © Robin Sheldon   Words: © Gordon Brattle

Away in a manger

Wootton

Words: verse 1, 2 unknown
verse 3 J T McFarland
Music: Paul Herrington

Copyright © Paul Herrington

12
VERSE 3 ARRANGEMENT

Come, light of the world

(Invocations)

for Music in Worship Trust

Words and music: Paul Inwood

Unison voices and keyboard.
Optional: guitars, SATB, vocal/instrumental descant, alternative instrumental descant, B♭ clarinet.

Words and music: © 1990 Paul Inwood
A & B Music, DABCEC, 4 Southgate Drive, Crawley, W Sussex RH10 6RP

16

world, be light for our eyes.
days, be strength for our minds.
world, bring warmth to our lives.
world, bring peace to us all.
God, in - spire all we do.

S.A.T.B. version

Sopranos sing the words of the verses, A.T.B. vocalise to 'ah'.

Vocal/Instrumental Descant

Alternative Instrumental Descant

Clarinet in B♭

Guide me, O my great Redeemer

Cwm Rhondda

Words: after W Williams,
P Williams and others
Music: J Hughes
Last verse arrangement and descant
Noël Tredinnick

1 Guide me, O my great Redeemer, pilgrim through this barren land;
  I am weak, but you are mighty, hold me with your powerful hand:
  Bread of heaven, bread of heaven, feed me now and evermore (evermore),
  feed me now and evermore!

2 O-pen now the crystal fountain where the healing waters flow;
  let the fiery, cloudy pillar lead me all my journey through:
  Strong Deliverer, strong Deliverer, ever be my strength and shield (strength and shield),
  ever be my strength and shield.

Orchestral parts compatible with this arrangement may be obtained from Laugham Arts,
2, All Souls Place, London W1N 3DB

Last verse arrangement and descant: © Noël H Tredinnick/Jubilate Hymns

LAST VERSE DESCANT

19

He is not dead

Words and music: Phil Rogers
arranged Roger Mayor

Orchestral backing track (cassette) and instrumental parts available from Music in Worship Trust.

Copyright © 1990 Phil Rogers, Thankyou Music, PO Box 75, Eastbourne BN23 6NW, UK. Used by permission.

Bb Trumpets or Clarinets

I will sing of your love and justice

for solo/choir and congregation

Misericordiam

Words: from Psalm 101,
Christopher Hayward
Music: Christopher Hayward

Glory

Words and music: Danny Daniels
Vocal arrangement David Peacock

This arrangement is primarily designed to be a vocal accompaniment by a worship group or choir, as the congregation sing the song. It is more effective when sung by memory.

Copyright © 1987 Mercy Publishing
Administered by Thankyou Music, PO Box 75, Eastbourne BN23 6NW, UK. Used by permission.

Lord, the light of your love

Festival arrangement for choir and congregation

Words and music: Graham Kendrick
arranged Roger Mayor

1 Lord, the light of your love is shin-ing, in the midst of the
2 Lord, I come to your awe-some pres-ence, from the sha-dows in-
3 As we gaze on your king-ly bright-ness so our fa-ces dis-

Ooh

Orchestral backing track (cassette) and instrumental parts available from Music in Worship Trust.

Words and music: © 1987 Make Way Music
Administered in Europe by Thankyou Music, PO Box 75, Eastbourne BN23 6NW, UK. Used by permission.

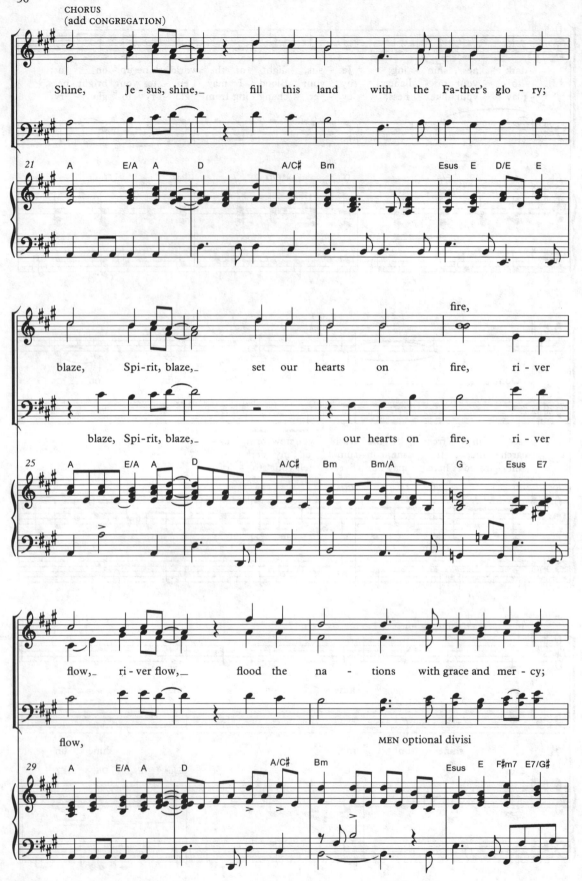

There is a green hill

To Maggie, David and Matthew

Words: Cecil F Alexander
Music: Paul Herrington

SOLO 1 There is a green hill far a-way,
WOMEN 2 We may not know we can-not tell
MEN 3 He died that we might be for-given,
SOLO 4 There was no o-ther good e-nough

out-side a ci-ty wall,
what pains he had to bear,
he died to make us good;
to pay the price of sin;

Copyright © Paul Herrington

42

Instrumental Obligato

Lord, you are the light of life

Fairmead

Words and music: Brian R Hoare
Verse 5 arrangement and
instrumental obligato Paul Herrington

1 Lord, you are the light of life to me; when darkness hides my path, you help me see. Shine on me, O Lord, that now and all my days your light may lead me on, guiding my ways.

2 Lord, (O, Lord!) you are the rock on which I stand, (I stand) stable and strong in you, held by your hand. Keep (O keep) me safe, O Lord, in weakness let there be (there be) your loving, firm embrace upholding me.

3 Lord, you are the truth that sets me free; only in you is found true liberty. Teach me then, O Lord, in all things to pursue your good and perfect will, growing like you.

4 Lord, you are the Lamb of God who died, suff'ring for love of me, scorned, crucified. Love me still, O Lord, let others daily see your selfless, serving love flowing through me.

Verse 1: UNISON
Verse 2: CHOIR
Verse 3: WOMEN UNISON
Verse 4: MEN UNISON

Copyright © Brian R Hoare/Jubilate Hymns

45

Instrumental Obligato

The Lord is my shepherd

Psalm of Faith

To Ruth and Dan
April 21 1990 Rochester Cathedral

Words: from Psalm 23, Ruth 1:16
Music: Norman Warren

Copyright © 1990 Norman Warren/Jubilate Hymns

48

Sing with joy
A fun song for families
for Music in Worship Trust

Words and music: Paul Inwood

*or 'morning'

Percussion instruments may well be added to this song,
and children could do actions to illustrate the more descriptive verses.

Copyright © 1990 Paul Inwood
A & B Music, DABCEC, 4 Southgate Drive, Crawley, W Sussex RH10 6RP

56

INTRO, INTERLUDE after each verse,
POSTLUDE at the end

OPTIONAL INSTRUMENT

Unto him who is able
(Benediction)

for Music in Worship Trust

Words and music: Roger Mayor

Orchestral backing track (cassette) and instrumental parts available from Music in Worship Trust.

Copyright © 1990 Roger Mayor/Jubilate Hymns

Seasonal and Settings Index

Advent
Come, light of the world

Christmas
Away in a manger
Come, light of the world
Glory
Lord, the light of your love

Easter
All heaven declares
Glory
He is not dead
Lord, you are light of life
There is a green hill

Pentecost
Come, light of the world
Lord, the light of your love

Harvest
Sing with joy

Communion
Come among us, Lord
Lord, you are the light of life
There is a green hill

General
Come among us, Lord
Come, light of the world
Glory
Guide me, O my great Redeemer
I will sing of your love and justice
Lord, you are the light of life
Lord, the light of your love
Sing with joy
The Lord is my shepherd
Unto him who is able

Anthems
All heaven declares
Come among us, Lord
Come, light of the world
Glory
Lord, you are the light of life
Lord, the light of your love
The Lord is my shepherd
There is a green hill
Unto him who is able

Worship Song Arrangements
All heaven declares
Glory
He is not dead
Lord, the light of your love
Sing with joy
Unto him who is able

Hymn Arrangements
Away in a manger
Guide me, O my great Redeemer
Lord, you are the light of life
There is a green hill

Descant
Guide me, O my great Redeemer

Suitable for use with Children
Away in a manger
He is not dead

Response Style
I will sing of your love and justice

SATB Settings
All heaven declares
Away in a manger
Come among us, Lord
Come, light of the world
Guide me, O my great Redeemer
Lord, you are the light of life
The Lord is my shepherd
There is a green hill

SAB Settings
Glory
He is not dead
Lord, the light of your love
Unto him who is able

Unison Settings
I will sing of your love and justice
Sing with joy (*for families*)